Leaving Teaching
By Clare Edwards

Copyright

Table of Contents

Introduction

'Saturdays weren't too bad but by Sunday I'd be getting anxious. I'd do some marking and planning, and then I'd try to unwind with a glass of wine but I would be worrying about work. By bedtime I'd start to feel slightly sick. I'd lay awake half the night thinking about my worst classes and the list of things I had to do.'
Nina
Before: Geography teacher
Now: Complimentary therapist

'Teaching, although rewarding, became too exhausting and too stressful with unrealistic targets and expectations from senior management as well as the pressure created by my own high standards.'
Chris
Before: Music teacher
Now: Private tutor

'After twenty years I felt like I'd done it all, seen it all. The same 'new' strategies would be reinvented and then pushed aside for the next big thing. I just thought - There must be something else, I've done this for too long.'
Lynn

Before: Primary school teacher
Now: Book keeping and accounts

Everyone gets frustrated at times, but for some people this is more than a passing phase and they really do start to think seriously about leaving teaching. Unfortunately, it isn't always easy. Perhaps you've browsed through the local paper or looked online for jobs near you. Did it come as a shock to realise that an assistant manager at a department store earns about half the wage of a Head of Department? Have you looked at jobs you might be interested in only to find that you don't appear to have the relevant experience to apply for them anyway?

We may complain about teachers' pay and conditions, but when you start to look at alternatives it can be daunting to realise that if you leave teaching, you will almost certainly have to accept less money, at least initially. Despite all your skills and experience, you will have to work to convince the non-teaching world that you can be successful. Fortunately, it can be done.

This book is for anyone considering leaving the teaching profession. You may be new to teaching, and have decided it's just not for you. Perhaps you are an experienced senior teacher who feels that the constant pressure to test, report and be observed has taken the joy out of the job.

Whatever your situation this book will help you think through the issues logically, enabling you to reach a decision based on sound research and honest reflection. It will look at a range of careers within education that you may not have considered. If you decide to leave teaching it will help you weigh up the alternatives realistically and put together a plan that will give you the best possible chance of success. It will even address the emotional impact of no longer being a teacher. Most importantly of all, the case studies in this book will show you that for many, many people, leaving teaching was one of the best decisions they ever made.

To get the most from this book I suggest you carry out the exercises which appear at the end of each chapter. These encourage you to think through your own personal circumstances. Have a notebook (paper or electronic) and spend time completing the exercises.

The research for this book was carried out using face to face interviews, telephone interviews, an on-line survey and social media. In total, information was collected from one hundred and twenty ex-teachers. Names and some details have been changed to preserve anonymity but the comments and case studies are all based on real people who have successfully left teaching.

Part One
Thinking it Through

Part one of this book will help you rationalise your thoughts about leaving teaching. If you've already made the decision that you definitely want to leave then you could skip this section and move on to part two. However, I don't recommend this. Even if you've made up your mind it will help to have your reasons clear so that you can communicate them to other people who may question your decision. You might find you have moments of doubt along the way and knowing that you've considered the situation from every angle will help dispel those doubts and stop you from worrying unnecessarily.

'I'd been stressed for a long time but I handed in my notice after an incident that I felt had been badly handled. It was a bit of a knee jerk reaction to be honest. Over the next two years there were lots of times when I thought I'd made a big mistake. Now I'm happily working elsewhere I'm glad I left, but I think if I'd thought it through more carefully I'd have been a bit more prepared.'
Meera
Before: Science teacher
Now: Assistant manager of clothes store

Chapter One
The Good, the Bad and the Paperwork

Teaching can be a fantastic job. It can also be soul destroying. In between those two extremes teaching can be a job which you once enjoyed but which may not be for you anymore. In many staff rooms in the country you'll find a small group of teachers complaining about how miserable they are, how badly behaved the children are these days and how useless the senior team is.

'Jerry used to moan all the time. He was a bit of a joke really. Then one day the Head announced that he was off sick and might be gone for 'some time'. The truth was he'd had a breakdown and was very ill for a long time. He never went back to teaching. I often thought how sad it was that he didn't get the support he needed, or that he didn't realise he'd had enough and leave before it made him ill.'
Gordon
Before: Sixth form maths teacher
Now: IT trainer

If you are deeply unhappy with your job, or feel that it's making you ill, you owe it yourself, your students, your colleagues and probably your family too to have a long hard look at your career and decide whether or not you need to take a new path.

Why teachers leave teaching
What makes a teacher want to leave teaching? Work load and stress are the two most commonly used terms, but there are plenty of other factors. Many teachers feel that are not being allowed to teach in the way they feel is best. This, coupled with what they see as unnecessary tasks, can lead to a deep sense of frustration.

'I get fed up of being asked to re-invent the wheel. I use small group teaching when it's the best way to teach a particular topic. I'm not going to start using it every lesson just because it's now got a fancy name.'
Angela
Now: Secondary Maths teacher

'I'm constantly being asked to do things which I don't feel are that important. Last term I spent a whole day on an equality and diversity course. My time would have been much better spent giving one to one support to some of my A level students but of course that's not seen as important.'
Jim
Now: Sixth Form Business Studies teacher

'There are no children in this school anymore. Each child now represents a percentage and my

job is to ensure the right percentage reach the specified target. Never mind if Jonny's dog died yesterday, can he order numbers to three decimal places?'
Hilary
Now: Primary school teacher

"If I'd wanted to do paperwork I'd have become a secretary."
Candy
Before: Primary school teacher
Now: Special needs teaching assistant

Occasionally, teachers will admit that they just don't feel up to the job.

'I plan fantastic lessons but I just can't get them to shut up long enough to tell them what to do. My behaviour management is terrible and although I've asked for support I know, in my heart of hearts, that I'm just not good enough.'
Kate
Now: Secondary English and drama teacher

Government figures for the UK show that approximately 45,000 teachers leave the profession before retirement age each year. New teachers are particularly vulnerable with estimates suggesting that up to 40% leave within the first five years. Although some of these may return to the profession, in England there are more than 230,000 qualified teachers of working

9

age who are not currently teaching. Below are some of the reasons given by teachers for their dissatisfaction with the job.

- Excessive work load
- Poor behaviour of students
- Lack of support from senior staff
- Too much focus on exam results and targets
- Bullying by the head or senior staff
- Changes to pay and pensions
- Too much paperwork
- Too many 'new' initiatives
- Unrealistic expectations of pupils' abilities
- Long hours during term time
- Poor work/life balance
- Verbal abuse from pupils
- Physical assault by student
- Not enough time to do things properly
- Too physically tiring
- Constant observations
- Criticism of performance
- Public perceptions
- Government interference
- Ofsted

Excessive workload is the number one reason given for teachers who have left or who want to leave teaching. Many teachers revealed that they regularly worked in excess of 60 hours a week during term time and some referred to the never ending nature of the job where there was always more that could be done.

'I always felt there was insufficient time to do what I considered to be a good job even though I was working 70 hours many weeks.'
Kim
Before: Primary school teacher
Now: Child minder

When teachers complain about an excessive work load they often receive little sympathy because, as we all know, the holidays are supposed to make up for the exhaustion you feel during term time. There is a tendency among teachers to work themselves to the limit during term time because they know the next holiday is never more than seven weeks away. This can lead to a very unhealthy attitude which completely destroys any work-life balance.

'It was great to have the holidays but life did feel like a roller-coaster where I was either working flat out or else I was in some kind of zombie state recovering. Now, I pace myself much better and I don't miss the holidays nearly as much as I thought I would.'

David
Before: FE lecturer
Now: Working for the Home Office

For many it isn't the hours they put in; it's the frustration that so much of what they are required to do feels like a waste of time.

'I thought the reason I hated teaching was the amount of hours I did, but to be honest, I put in far more hours in the eighteen months after I left when I went self-employed. The difference was that I didn't resent sitting up till three in the morning to meet a deadline for a contract I'd won, whereas I did mind sitting up till three in the morning writing a detailed report on my department's results which I was pretty sure no one would read.'
Marcus
Before: Head of Modern Foreign Languages department
Now: Company translator

A lack of support from senior teachers is another common theme, and accusations of bullying cropped up surprisingly often. It appears that once a teacher has fallen out of favour with the Head or senior team they can often come in for extra scrutiny and criticism.

'I was badly bullied by the Head Teacher and my Head of Department. This was supported by a

number of teachers in the school who colluded with it.'
Alison
Before: Teacher of modern foreign languages
Now Private tutor

One ex-teacher felt that although bullying was a hot topic when it came to pupil behaviour, some schools had an underlying culture of bullying within the staff structure.

'In all three schools I worked in I felt the senior team made unreasonable demands on staff, and then became distinctly cool towards anyone who didn't bend over backwards to try to meet those demands. It ranged from the downright childish – a teacher given an extra break duty for example, to outright discrimination – a prolonged restructuring process which ended with a redundancy which was actually a foregone conclusion.'
Will
Before: History teacher
Now: Hypnotherapist

One topic which comes up repeatedly when asking ex-teachers why they left teaching is the stress caused by Ofsted, lesson observations, targets and performance management in general. Of course teachers have to be accountable but some people felt they were being held accountable for things over which they had no control. Others felt that the drive for constant improvement drove out the true purpose of teaching. Many felt unfairly judged.

'I went into teaching in my forties and taught maths in a large comprehensive. I loved the job and for the first two years everyone seemed very happy with me. Then we had Ofsted. The inspector saw 20 minutes of my lesson and gave me a 3 – requires improvement. After that I found myself under intense scrutiny. I had extra observations which all came out as 3's even though I'd had 1's and 2's before. The senior team looked at my marking and there was talk of putting me on an improvement programme. I handed in my notice and left at the end of the school year. When the exam results came out my two classes had the second best results in the department. Only the Head of Department's class had done better. I'm now teaching abroad in a job I absolutely love where my judgement is trusted. The whole experience of Ofsted and what happened afterwards nearly put an end to my career. I think if I'd been younger I would have gone under.'
Frank
Before: Maths teacher
Now: Maths teacher abroad

Intense scrutiny and the requirement to justify everything they did was another frequently cited.

'I was a primary school teacher for 22 years on and off. My first Head would wander into the classroom about once a week, leaf through a few project books, watch from the back for five minutes then wander out again. When I left he wrote me a detailed reference which showed that he'd been aware of just about everything I did. My last Head asked for mid term lesson plans for every subject and detailed lesson plans whenever the whim took him. There were three formal lesson observations every year and I had to write a report on my class for the governors each term. He returned my performance management document to me three times because it didn't include enough detail. I really resented the idea that doing the job wasn't good enough – I had to prove I was doing it too.'
Anna
Was: Primary school teacher
Now: NVQ trainer and assessor

For some ex-teachers schools simply don't live up to their idea of what teaching should be about.

'Too much bureaucracy got in the way of teaching. I went into education because I thought it was about growing children into the best adults they could be. I thought it was about helping children to reach their full potential in every aspect of their lives. I thought it was about growing confident, happy children with a thirst for learning into confident happy adults with

high self-esteem. I discovered it was more about reaching arbitrary targets set by people who had never met my pupils. It was about cramming children full of facts that they found irrelevant to their lives and did not help them find meaning in the world. It was about league tables and writing reports. I could no longer work in an environment that I found stifling to children's creative sense of self.'

Lorie
Before: Science teacher
Now: Psychotherapist, supervisor and trainer

You may well identify with many of the concerns mentioned above, but you probably have your own reasons for thinking about leaving teaching as well.

The three exercises below are all designed to help you think about your attitude to teaching and how you feel about your current job. You have probably already spent many hours thinking about your job but it might help to look at it a little more subjectively. Spend some time doing any or all of the exercise before thinking about the final question at the end of this chapter.

Exercise one
What don't you like?
Write down all the things you dislike about your job. Include everything from the large philosophical differences you may have with

teaching to the small, irritating things. Don't censor your thoughts, just write.

This is a good exercise to start with because your head is probably already full of things you don't like about teaching. It may have been going round and round in your brain for some time. Get it all down on paper where you can see it.

When you've finished, have a look at your list. You'll probably find that it contains a combination of 'opinions' and 'tasks'. Opinions include things like 'I don't like the way students speak to me', and tasks might include 'marking.' Try to be aware of how many of the things you don't like are your opinions about the job and how many are things you have to do.

For the moment focus on the opinions on your list. Can you change your way of thinking about any of them?

'I spent several years railing against how things were and what should be different. One day, an older colleague told me I'd wear myself out worrying about things I couldn't change. It made a huge difference. Now, I just accept that schools aren't ideal and a lot of what goes on probably shouldn't but that's just how it is. I've stopped expecting my Head of Faculty to behave differently; she's never going to. It's amazing how tolerant I've become. I think maybe half my stress was self-inflicted.'
Angela

Now: Secondary Maths teacher

Another useful way of reflecting on how you feel about your job is to draw a distinction between the things you do as part of your job, and the things which get done to you. Many people, when they complete the above exercise find that a significant number of the things they don't like about their job are things which are done to them Examples might include having your lessons observed or senior staff not backing you when students misbehave. If you find that most of the things you don't like about teaching are actually the things you have to do as part of your job, (e.g. planning lessons, marking, speaking to parents, writing reports) then you are one step nearer to deciding that teaching is not for you. If, on the other hand, most of the things you don't like seem to be more to do with how other people run the school, then the situation is more complicated. It could be that it's your particular school causing the problem rather than teaching itself. We'll return to this thought in chapter two.

Keep hold of your list. We'll be coming back to it later.

Exercise two
What do you actually do?
Write a list of everything you do at work. This will be a long list. Include as much detail as you can, for example 'teaching lessons' might be broken down into:

- Greeting and settling the class
- Taking register
- Giving whole class instructions
- Using audio visual resources
- Asking questions
- Answering questions
- Helping groups or individual pupils
- Marking work with pupils
- Challenging poor behaviour

You can probably think of more. Continue writing your list for every aspect of your job. It might help to take the list to work with you for a few days and add to it as you go along.

When your list is as complete as you can make it you can start to evaluate what you actually do all day. Get your highlighters out and identify the things you enjoy, the things you don't enjoy and the things which cause you real stress. Roughly how long do you spend each day doing the things you enjoy or feel are worthwhile? Are these things spoilt by the fact that you never have the time to finish them properly, or perhaps you feel other people don't value them? Try to get to the bottom of what it is you dislike about your job. Is there a way of changing any of it?

Exercise three
Why did you choose teaching ?
Think about the following questions. Write the answers down if that helps.

1. What made you choose a career in teaching?
2. Who played a role in your decision to become a teacher and how?
3. Did you consider any other careers?
4. What did you expect to enjoy about teaching?
5. If you had to pick just one reason, what would you say was your main reason for becoming a teacher?

Remember this isn't interview preparation. You are talking to yourself so don't pretend you were desperate to influence young minds if the real reason you chose teaching was because you loved sport but you weren't good enough to be a professional footballer or that you liked the idea of the holidays. On the other hand, do try to remember any noble thoughts you did have. You will probably find that your reasons were a mix of altruistic and practical motives. Think hard and really try to uncover all the things which influenced you. Did you secretly picture yourself becoming the youngest head teacher in Britain standing in assembly while 500 eager little faces gazed up at you in awe? You may have harboured highly ambitious or idealistic dreams which seem a naïve to you now. There is a place for idealism in teaching. It's easy to get jaded and it might be that thinking back to why you wanted to teach in the first place might help point you in the direction you need to take next.

When you have finished answering the questions in exercise three take time to think about how your attitude to teaching has changed over the years. Is it a change for the better or worse? What do you think has caused that change?

The first decision – Do you want to leave your job?

By now you should be beginning to have a clearer picture of how you feel about teaching and your present job at the moment. If you completed all three exercises you will have thought about what you don't like, looked closely at what you actually do and remembered why you became a teacher in the first place. You should now be in a fairly strong position to answer the following question:

Do you want to leave your job? At this point don't think about whether you can afford to leave your job, or whether you should. Just answer the question – Do you want to?

Chapter Two
Fed up with Teaching or just this Particular Job?

A change of school

Sometimes it's the particular job and not the career that's the problem.

'I was in my first school for five years. I left because the Head was a bully. I stayed in the second school for 8 years and then did 2 years in another school. All three were different. The last school was the best school I ever worked in. I left because I was made redundant.'

Alison
Before: Teacher of modern foreign languages
Now Private tutor

Look back at your lists from the first two exercises again. Could most of the things you dislike be peculiar to your particular establishment? For example, there are massive amounts of paperwork in every school but some are more efficient than others. The way behaviour is managed varies from school to school and the expectations of staff are often different.

'On paper, this school and my first school are very similar – similar size, similar results,

similar types of catchment areas – but they feel completely different. I have to produce the same paperwork but there's a clear timetable for when things are due so I can plan properly. Meetings don't run over or get changed at the last minute so I can organise my own child care easily. And senior staff listen if there's a problem and make useful suggestions rather than sighing and telling you everyone has the same problem.'
Jill
Now: English teacher

'I hated my first job. I was inexperienced, there was no support and it was quite rough. I wanted to leave teaching but I couldn't find another job so I took a temporary post in another school. I was dreading it and I nearly didn't turn up on the first day. Turned out to be a totally different experience – I loved it from day one! I ended up staying for six years and although I've moved now I'll always be grateful that I found myself there. My advice would be, all schools are different, just because you hate one doesn't mean you'll hate them all.'
Carole
Now: Food Technology teacher

This is probably good advice, especially for new teachers. A first post can sometimes be a real challenge and many teachers who found their first year almost unbearable find they start to manage more easily in their second year. If you're really unhappy in your first school then it would be worth trying somewhere else before you decide that teaching is not for you. A new start somewhere else could make all the difference.

'I learnt a lot in my first job but by the end of the year I'd already got the reputation for being the weak new teacher and I didn't feel I could overcome it. In my second school I was able to start with confidence and the job was just much easier.'
Helen
Before: English and drama teacher.
Now: Class teacher in a school for pupils with Severe Learning Difficulties.

A change of role
If you completed exercise two in the first chapter you will have identified whether or not the things you dislike about teaching would apply to any teaching post. If most of the things on your list are things which are integral to teaching then this is a pretty good indication that you need to find a new career. If, however, there were many things on your list which you do enjoy, but which you feel you don't do enough of then a change of role rather than a change of career might be worth a try. Could you negotiate a new role in your current school, or apply for a different role somewhere else?

'I had been a Head of Sixth form for three years. Everyone saw me as the sympathetic, kind type who worked well with parents and children with problems, but to be honest, I got sick to death of teenagers coming to me with their problems! I just wanted to teach. After speaking to the Head he agreed to a reshuffle and I moved from being a head of year to being the second in the English department. I had a bigger teaching load and less money but I was much happier.'
Christine
Before: Head of Sixth form
Now: Assistant Leader of English Faculty

Moving from a senior position to a less senior position is quite common.

'Over the course of 25 years I went from being a classroom teacher, up through head of department then assistant head, then back to classroom teacher. It seemed like a natural progression and although I liked having senior posts being back in the classroom full time means you can ignore a lot of the politics.'
Jenny
Before: Assistant Head
Now: French and German teacher

A different type of teaching
A large percentage of teachers who leave the mainstream classroom remain in education in some form or other. In some ways, this is an

easier transition that leaving teaching altogether and financially you may be better off. Special schools are an obvious area to consider.

'When I'm at work I work harder than ever before. You never know how the young people are going to behave and you're on duty every break time and right through lunch. There's also plenty of paperwork and we get Ofsted just the same but I don't take home anywhere near as much work. I only have six in a class so the marking is minimal and because it's 14 to 16 I only have one key stage to plan for. I would say I do more planning as you have to really capture their imagination and have alternatives up your sleeve for when they refuse to do something but I get most of my planning done midweek. I no longer spend every Sunday marking GCSE and A level essays.'
Sally.
Before: English teacher.
Now: Residential school for children with Emotional, Behavioural and Social Difficulties

'I used to teach Drama and English in a large comprehensive. The KS3 pupils had one 35 minute lesson a week and I taught over 350 children. By the end of the year I still didn't know all their names. Now I have eight children. I know their names, birthdays, favourite foods, families, pets, medication, physio needs and

speech therapy programmes to name just some of it! You know you matter in a special school.'
Helen
Before: English and drama teacher.
Now: Class teacher in a school for pupils with Severe Learning Difficulties.

A change of age group can also feel like a new career.

'I retrained as a Primary teacher after 12 years of teaching in secondary. Initially the workload was enormous but three years in I'm much happier. I like having my own class and having total responsibility for them for a whole year. You get to know them really well and I love their enthusiasm. I wouldn't say they were easier than teenagers but it is easier to build up a relationship with them.'
Rob
Before: Secondary science teacher
Now: Primary school teacher

Most of us have family commitments which limit where we can work. If this is not the case for you perhaps you would consider teaching abroad.

'Four years ago I was at rock bottom. Newly divorced, both children left home and a job in a school I hated. One morning I thought, I don't have to do this anymore. I applied for a job at an International school in the Middle East and three

months later I was on the plane. Although I was terrified, it turned out to be the best thing I've ever done. I'd forgotten how much I loved teaching. It was a joy to have small classes of children who really wanted to learn. The weather was a big bonus too! I stayed for three years and after that I moved back to England and I now just do supply when I need to. I made so many good friends and have such great memories. I'd recommend it to anyone.'
Janet
Before: History teacher
Now: Supply teacher

Another option is to move from the state sector to the private sector. Independent schools are likely to have smaller classes, but the expectations will be just as high.

'I used to teach in a pupil referral unit. Then I had an accident and was off work for a long time. After that, I didn't feel I had the energy to return to the PRU and I got a job in a small independent school so in a sense I went from one extreme to another. The actual teaching was not that different – once children are immersed in an art project they tend to need the same thing – encouragement and praise. I sometimes miss the excitement of the PRU and the money is less but all in all it was the right decision for me.'
Cheryl
Before: Art teacher at a pupil referral unit

Now: Art teacher at an independent school

'I taught in a comprehensive for two years then, being young free and single, I went to Peru to teach. I met my wife out there and we decided to return to England. I'd loved being part of the wider life of a boarding school in Peru so I got a job in a boarding school in England. Although I teach science I also go sailing, do evening duties and am involved with the cadets. We live on site and during term time it does feel like you're on duty 24 hours a day but I don't mind that. It's more of a lifestyle than a career.'
Philip
Before: Science teacher in an international school abroad
Now: Head of science in an independent boarding school

Exercise four
Would a new school or role be the answer?
Go back to the list you made in exercise one of the things you don't like about your job. How many of the things you don't like would apply to teaching in any situation and how many of them are specific to your particular school or role? It might help to do the same exercise with the items on your list from exercise two as well. Spend some time focusing on the things in the second list that you do like about teaching. Are there any that you could do more of if only you were teaching somewhere else? For example, if your

relationship with the students is the thing you like best, would you consider working in a special school or a pupil referral unit? If your A level class is the best class of the week would a move into some form of higher education be worthwhile?

Exercise five
What else is out there?
You probably think you know your area quite well but you may find that there are several organisations that you are not even aware of. This is especially true if all your job searches have been confined to the LEA website. Decide on a reasonable travelling distance and carry out a thorough internet search to uncover all the educational providers in that area. One useful way of doing this is to use the Ofsted website. Ofsted currently inspects a huge variety of education providers and you can do a search of all providers within a 20 mile radius of any postcode. You might discover units attached to children's homes, private special schools, post 16 training providers and others you haven't thought of. If any organisation catches your eye then it might be worth finding out more about them and perhaps arranging a visit. There may be no jobs going there at the moment but it doesn't hurt to show you face and get a feel for a place.

Chapter Three
When you Have No Choice

Sometimes teaching careers come to an end not through choice but through circumstances. You may have moved to an area where there are just no jobs, or you may have other commitments which prevent you from taking up regular work. Recent legislation means that it is far easier to remove unsatisfactory teachers. In reality, many choose to jump before they're pushed.

'I'd been teaching tech for 16 years. Under the old framework I usually got 3's for my observations – satisfactory. I was fine with that. My lessons were a bit old fashioned but the kids enjoyed them and made progress. To me, tech was all about giving students a chance to do something new and be proud of what they produced. Then the new framework came in and 3 suddenly became 'requires improvement.' At about the same time we got a new Head. Everyone was observed and anyone on a 3 was put on an improvement programme. I did my best but it knocked my confidence and I lost all faith in my ability to teach. Also, the 'support' I got was all over the place. I could show the same lesson plan to two different senior teachers and one would say it was really good and the other would say it wasn't good enough. I knew that if I

didn't improve, in their eyes, I'd be looking at capability. I couldn't sleep and I stopped eating properly. At the same time my wife was ill and needed a lot of care. I contacted my union and in the end, after negotiating with the Head, I agreed to resign as a teacher and work instead as a teaching assistant. Although I did feel a bit of a failure it was a huge relief. It meant taking a big pay cut but once you take tax into consideration I had more left than I thought I would. Besides, it was more than I would have got if I'd lost my job completely. It was definitely the right decision given the circumstances but I do wonder if I could have carried on teaching if the ethos of the place had been different.'

Jack
Before: Technology teacher
Now: Teaching assistant

If you're thinking of leaving teaching because of performance issues, make sure you seek advice from your union before you make any decisions. Never hand your notice in because you feel under pressure.

'I'd had a lot of time off sick and the Head started talking about capability. I handed my notice in rather than face that. After six months off my health improved and I felt ready to teach again. I applied for quite a few jobs and had a couple of interviews but no one would employ me. In the end I signed up with a supply agency and after a

few months one of the schools I worked at offered me a full time post so everything was ok but I wish I'd taken advice at the time. I was ill, I shouldn't have been treated as an incompetent teacher.'
Jill
Now: English teacher

Whilst you shouldn't be put under any pressure to resign due to ill health, you may feel that the job itself is contributing to your illness. Again, it is important to receive support and advice. Contact occupational health if there are any health issues which are making it difficult for you to do your job. Your school has to support you and occupational health should ensure they make any reasonable adjustments that are needed. Even so, you may decide, after receiving support and advice, that you need to leave teaching for the sake of your health.

'I was constantly stressed. I loved the job – perhaps too much – and I wanted everything to be perfect. I worked over 60 hours a week and quite a bit of the holidays too. Looking back, I suppose I was a workaholic. I started getting migraines then heart palpitations and eventually full blown panic attacks. My doctor felt it was due to the constant stress I was putting myself under. Lots of people tried to get me to slow down but I couldn't. I think it was my own fault really – even the Head said I worked too hard.

For a while I tried to limit the work I did but that made me feel worse – I still couldn't relax but now I felt I wasn't doing a good job either. Eventually I decided that teaching was going to kill me. I took a break and did some voluntary work and through that was offered a job with a charity. I miss teaching but it became a monster!'

Heather
Before: Primary school teacher
Now: Regional fund raising manager of national charity

'I had constant back problems and had so much time off work it just didn't seem fair to anyone. I tried part time but even that was too much. Teaching just isn't a job where you can go and lay down for ten minutes when you need to.'

Colin
Before: Secondary PE teacher
Now: Part time sales manager

Some teacher's careers come to an end due to a specific incident.

'I was the victim of a false accusation made by a child who didn't like being told off and so invented lies. It took five months to clear my name. The child remained at the school and I couldn't face going back. The LEA didn't want the bother of prosecuting the child or parents, and I got no support from the new Head who

was watching her back and trying to build a name for herself for 'turning around a failing school'. After being off ill with stress for nearly a year I accepted voluntary redundancy.'
Tina
Before: Geography teacher
Now: Currently unemployed

'I was a Primary Head for five years. We went through a difficult time and I was approached by an Academy chain who wanted to take us over. It looked like a good opportunity and they seemed keen to work with me. In less than a year of becoming an Academy we had a poor Ofsted and I was 'invited' to leave. I applied for a number of other senior posts but got nothing. I was told by one of the employment agencies that 'you're only as good as your last Ofsted'. Eventually I was offered a class teaching job in a special needs school. It was the best thing that could have happened to me and I absolutely love it.'
Hannah
Before: Primary Head
Now: Special needs teacher

Being in a position where you feel you have no choice but to leave teaching is not a nice position to be in. At some level you may feel relief that you won't have to teach again but this may also be mixed with feelings of failure, worthlessness, injustice, anger, helplessness and any number of

37

additional uncomfortable feelings. If possible, try to remember that your working life does not define who you are as a person. Whether or not you feel you bear some fault in what has happened, work is only one part of your life; it's what you do not who you are. Look for support and accept it when it's offered. The Teacher's Support Line is a really good place to start. Take heart too from other people who've been in your position and have lived through it.

'I made a serious error of judgement and as a result I lost my job. At the time I thought I'd never be able to leave the house again but you'd be amazed how quickly people forget, or at least, cease to care. A very kind relative offered me a job in her business and I'm now a partner. I can look back now and think, yes, I was an idiot, but in the grand scheme of things the only person who got hurt was me and I survived. It's made me a more tolerant person – I know that people make mistakes but you can't change the past and you have to move on. If anyone had said that to me at the time I would probably have wanted to punch them but it's true. In the end, you just have to lift your head high and get on with your life.'
Anne
Before: Drama teacher
Now: Partner in events planning company

Exercise six
Look after yourself and consult the experts
If you've been forced out of teaching think about taking the advice of someone else who's been in that position.

'For the first few months after I left all I could think about was what had happened. I went over and over it constantly in my head, replaying conversations or having imaginary conversations where I managed to come out better. I knew it wasn't healthy but I couldn't help it. I was also very short of money and any job I looked at was so badly paid I didn't know how I'd manage. In the end I made three promises to myself.
Firstly, I made myself limit the time I spent thinking about what had happened. I arranged some counselling through the Teachers' Support Line and on top of that I allowed myself to think about it for only half an hour a day. After that I would make myself stop and think about something else. Limiting it really helped.
Secondly, I decided to apply for every job I could and take the first one I was offered. It meant I worked in a coffee shop for six months but it got me out of the house and gave me something else to think about.
And thirdly, I spent time every day doing something creative or something active.

Those three things kept me sane. I got chatting to someone at the coffee shop who gave me an idea for a whole new career and that's what I'm doing now.'

Paula

Before: Teaching Functional Skills in a college of Further Education

Now: Self-employed accountancy and book keeping

If you are thinking of leaving teaching because you feel under pressure don't make any decisions until you have spoken to your doctor, your union, Occupational Health and the Teacher Support Agency at the very least. Make the appointments today.

Chapter Four
What's it Like to Not to be a Teacher?

For most teachers being a teacher is central to their lives and to their view of themselves. Although they may feel that the Government, students, parents or the public in general don't think highly enough of teachers, there is a certain camaraderie about being a teacher. In any social situation where the talk turns to careers, when you say you're a teacher it will always evoke a response. Everyone has an opinion about teachers. There is also that recognition between teachers which is usually cause for a few wry comments and when you meet other teachers you know there is a shared understanding of many aspects of the job. It can feel like being part of a club and when you are no longer a teacher it can leave a hole in your life which, if you're not careful, can leave you feeling that there is a hole in your identity.

'For years when people asked what I'd say 'I used to be a teacher, but now I have a little company that does wedding planning.' I don't know why I played down the wedding planning company, I was actually very proud of it and it was soon a good business. I think, in the back of

my mind, I had this feeling that wedding planning wasn't as worthy as teaching and I didn't deserve to be proud of it. Now I just say I'm a wedding planner, but it took me about three years.'

Laura
Before: Home Economics teacher
Now: Wedding planner

'I felt I lost status somehow. As a teacher I used to feel no one had any respect for the profession, but once I was working in sales it was worse.'

Colin
Before: Secondary PE teacher
Now: Sales manager

'I didn't know what to do with myself. My husband had a good job and I didn't really need to work but I felt adrift, like I didn't have a purpose in life. And I missed interacting with people and being creative and that buzz you get when you've got too much to do. I started doing voluntary work as a way of feeling useful again.'

Heather
Before: Primary school teacher
Now: Regional fund raising manager of national charity

It's possible that other people will see you differently too, although perhaps not as much as you would think.

'I do often feel that people look down on me a bit now that I'm a child minder and I find myself justifying why I left teaching.'
Kim
Before: Primary school teacher
Now: Child minder

'I felt terrible when I left teaching. Suddenly I was earning half the money and I had this feeling that I'd let my partner down. Instead of having a career I was proud of, I just had a poorly paid job. Even though my partner had supported my decision to leave, I still worried about what he thought. I tried to over compensate by redecorating the house and cooking complicated meals. In the end he pointed out that I'd left teaching because of the stress and now I was just creating more for the sake of it.'
Meera
Before: Science teacher
Now: Assistant manager of clothes store

Feelings of failure are common, even if you are sure you've made the right decision.

'There is a bit of me, a big bit of me that still feels I didn't try hard enough and that if I'd been a better teacher I could have carried on. Maybe that's true but you can't beat yourself up for ever.'
Jack
Before: Technology teacher

Now: Teaching assistant

It's worth thinking ahead about how you will cope if you experience low moments when you look back and wonder whether teaching was quite as bad as you remember it. Keep the lists you made in chapter one just in case you ever need to remind yourself of the reasons you left in the first place.

Because teaching tends to be an all-encompassing profession many teachers find that their social lives are closely linked to colleagues and former colleagues. If most of your friends are teachers, if your partner is a teacher or if many of your family members are teachers, leaving teaching can be even more difficult.

'There were four of us who used to work in the same school and we became firm friends. We all moved on to other jobs but we'd still meet regularly for a drink and go away for weekends together. The other three stayed in teaching but I moved into social work. I did find after a while that being with them was less enjoyable because the talk often centred around teaching and education. Occasionally I would think, well, if you do a bad job, someone might fail an exam, if I do a bad job someone could die. I never felt they really understood my job.'
Marnie
Before: Careers adviser in residential school
Now: Social worker

Of course, no one stays in a career they don't like just to keep friends, but it's important not to underestimate how much not being a teacher may change your life.

Vast numbers of ex-teachers regard the change as largely positive though, and many of the ways in which not being a teacher changes your life are clearly beneficial. All of the items below have been identified by ex-teachers as being benefits they gained from leaving teaching.

- Less stress
- Shorter working hours
- More family time
- Better quality family time
- A more reasonable working week
- A better work/life balance
- Improved social life
- Improved health
- Sleeping better
- Don't feel bullied
- Can leave work at work
- Greater sense of achievement
- No longer dread going back to work after the weekend or holiday
- Look forward to work
- Feel more valued
- Better working conditions

- Able to take breaks during the working day
- Greater sense of independence
- No longer feel at the mercy of the whims of those above me
- Increased pride in my work
- No Ofsted

This comment is typical of many:

'I have a much better quality of life now; I am far less stressed and enjoy what I do.'
Chris
Before: Music teacher
Now: Private tutor

Exercise seven
How will you feel?
Think about how your life would be different if you left teaching. Make sure you consider the negatives as well as the positives. How will you cope with the negatives? What impact will it have on your sense of identity?

Chapter Five
Can you Afford to Leave?

Thinking about retirement

Whatever age you are, it's worth finding out where you stand in terms of retirement age and your pension. The days when teachers could retire on a good pension at 50 are long gone, and there have been so many changes both to the retirement age and pension arrangements that it is impossible to give general advice. The majority of teachers have a pension with the Teachers Pension Scheme. You can register online with them (www.teacherspensions.co.uk) to see exactly what pension contributions you have made so far and what age you can claim your pension. They can also give you a forecast of what your pension is worth. If you have any questions they are very helpful. It is worth checking your employment history from time to time as it is relatively common for employers to miss recording pension contributions and your pension will be affected if you have periods of service missing. If you think there has been a mistake you should contact the employer you were working for at the time. The sooner you spot mistakes the easier it is to correct them.

'When I was 58 I checked my pension record and found that there were three years missing from over ten years ago. Luckily I had payslips still

and actually I didn't need them as the Local Authority I worked for then sorted it out straight away but I'm glad I checked as it did make a difference to my pension.'
Roy
Before: Maths teacher
Now: Happily retired

Whether or not you decide to leave teaching, a session with an independent financial adviser to look at your pension arrangements is worth considering as there are lots of options including making additional payments which may be of benefit to you. You might also want to look at the rules regarding working past pension age, and working part time after you start receiving your pension if you think this might apply to you. The citizen's advice bureau has a useful section on how to find an independent financial adviser. Your Union may also be able to put you in touch with a financial adviser.

In addition to this, you should seek advice from your doctor, union and HR department if you think you would be eligible for early retirement on the grounds of ill health.

If retirement is not an option then a major factor in your decision to leave or remain in teaching is your financial situation.

The hard truth about leaving teaching
Financial well-being was the only area in the research for this book where the majority of

teachers reported that their circumstances had got worse. That's probably not what you wanted to hear, but it's a fact. Ex-teachers tend to fall into four camps and of these, only one group regularly reported being financially better off as ex-teachers than when they had been teachers.

1. The first group consisted largely of parents (and they were mostly women) who chose to leave teaching when their children were small. Often these people returned to work part time to avoid paying for full time child care for their own children. Their earnings were therefore less than their salaries when they were teaching.

2. Teachers who had been in the profession for a while, typically between 8 and 20 years, had a hard time finding work which was as well paid as their teaching careers. Most of these teachers had received promotions and increments meaning that they were some way up the teachers' pay scale when they left. Although some of these teachers eventually matched their previous earnings, it often took more than five years.

3. Teachers who left teaching towards the end of their careers, having taught for 25

or more years, rarely earned as much in their new careers as they had as teachers. This is partly explained by the fact that they were often high up on the teachers' pay scale or leadership scale when they left. But it is also due to the fact that many of these ex-teachers did not feel the need to earn as much as they had before. Some had partners who were high earners and many simply didn't need to earn as much. These ex-teachers had often paid off their mortgages and most no longer had dependent children. Their decision to leave teaching was made easier by the fact that they could afford to take a reduction in income.

4. The only group of ex-teachers who consistently reported an improved financial position were those who left the profession early, generally within the first five years of qualifying. Most of these reported a dip in earnings to begin with but were able to regain and even exceed their previous earnings within a few years.

There are always exceptions but realistically it's best to assume that you will face a drop in income if you decide to leave teaching. For many the benefits outweigh this disadvantage, considerable though it is.

'As a child minder I only earn about half what I earned as a teacher but it's definitely worth it. We've had to make sacrifices; we don't holiday abroad now and I sometimes worry that we're not saving any money but I'm happier, more relaxed and I'm able to take and pick up my own daughter from school which is important to me.'
Kim
Before: Primary school teacher
Now: Child minder

'I felt trapped in teaching because we relied on my earnings. I thought I couldn't afford to give up. In the end, it was affecting me so badly my wife sat me down and said, whatever it takes, you need to leave. We put into place every cost cutting measure we could think of. It's meant we haven't been able to help the children out as much as I would have liked but I've been surprised at how little we've missed the money really. When you're happy, as long as you're not starving, you don't mind having less.'
Simon
Before: Senior teacher and maths teacher
Now: Handyman and gardener

What you can expect to earn
When we compare average earnings in the UK, we can see why some teachers feel they can't afford to stop teaching. According to figures published by the Office for National Statistics the average salary for teaching and educational

professionals in 2012 was £32,105. There are plenty of occupations with higher average earnings, for example solicitor £45,585, quantity surveyor £38,150 or even air traffic controllers £63,855, but clearly all of these require considerable investment in terms of retraining and gaining experience. If we look at jobs which the average teacher might be able to apply for with minimal training we get a very different picture:

- Driving instructor £29,844
- Customer services manager £29,565
- Estate agent £26,889
- Prison service officer £25,846
- Office supervisor £25,054
- Careers adviser £23,624
- Coach driver £22,411
- Book keeper and wages clerk £20,736
- Telesales person £17,533
- Receptionist £12,344
- Retail assistant £9,742
- Cleaner £7,894

Average salaries are not particularly helpful given that, as someone new to a profession or career, you would be going in towards the bottom, so let's look at actual jobs you might be able to apply for.

The following jobs were all advertised in August 2014. They are all full time jobs.

- Stockroom assistant £13,806
- University campus porter £12,960
- Telesales adviser £12,800
- Customer adviser for a national bank £12,800-£16,000
- IT support officer £17,353

A number of jobs would seem well paid and suitable for ex-teachers until you look at the experience required. The job of student recruitment and communications officer at a large university would seem an ideal ex-teacher's job and offers a salary of £26,000. When you look at the experience required however, it includes:

- Detailed knowledge of Customer Relationship Management
- Experience of co-ordinating design and print projects
- Proven experience of successfully using online platforms to deliver events and interactive communications.

The average teacher might struggle to meet these criteria. This advert also highlights the need to understand industry specific terms and jargon. As a teacher, you bandy about acronyms and buzz words which many non-teachers would struggle to identify, but as a newcomer to communications you may not have spotted that by 'online platform for interactive communication' they probably mean a webinar.

Of course there are some golden opportunities for ex-teachers which offer pretty good rewards. Most senior teachers who have been in a management position would have been able to apply for the role of campus manger with a large adult education provider which offered a salary of £38,000. But jobs of this sort are not very frequent and are highly sought after.

The information above is not given to make you dispirited. Remember approximately 45,000 teachers in the UK each year do leave teaching, and not all of them starve. There are ways to increase your chances of leaving teaching and still earn a good income, and we will look at these later on. For the present, you need to really think about whether or not your desire to leave teaching is strong enough or urgent enough for you to consider taking a drop in salary.

'I complained constantly about teaching and eventually I started a serious job search to see if there were alternatives out there. I quickly found that I would struggle to match my current salary, even if I was prepared to retrain. I knew of a colleague who'd been very successful setting up his own business but I also knew of the hours he'd put in and the risk he'd taken re-mortgaging

his house. In the end, I decided I was better off staying where I was. Once I'd made the decision I stopped complaining. I figured I either needed to get out or get on with it and since I didn't really have the motivation to get out I just got on with it.'
Mike
Now: Primary deputy head

Exercise eight
How much income do you need?
There are lots of online calculators and websites to help you work out a realistic budget. Moneysavingexpert.com has a good budget planner and so does the Money Advice Service. Use one of these to calculate what you currently spend each month and what you could afford to cut. This should give you an idea of what you need to earn to stay afloat.

Exercise nine
How badly do you want out?
Write a list of things you currently spend your money on which you don't physically need to survive. Sort them into a rough order starting with the ones you wouldn't really miss and ending with the ones that you can't imagine life without. How far down your list are you prepared to go in order to get out of the classroom? What other life changes would you be prepared to make to achieve your aim of leaving teaching? Would you be prepared to move to a smaller house? Move to

a cheaper part of the country? Move in with your in-laws? Of course you have to balance your needs against those of the rest of your family but you're really only required to feed, clothe and shelter your children, anything else is negotiable. And whilst they might complain bitterly about having to share a bedroom, would it be worth it if they gain a happier parent?

Many people feel trapped in teaching because they don't believe they can survive on less money. In truth, there are many families who survive on much lower than a teacher's wage. When you say you can't afford to give up teaching, what you are really saying is that you and your family are not prepared to take the drop in lifestyle which that might require. There is nothing wrong with that, but be honest about your reasons for staying in teaching. If you accept that your job is what is allowing you to live the way you do then you might decide that it's worth it.

Do you want to leave teaching?
If you've read this far and done all the recommended thinking you should be in a pretty good position to make the major decision now. Do you want to leave teaching? That doesn't necessarily mean leaving education altogether and we'll come back to that in the next section.

So far you have:

- Thought about what you like and dislike about teaching, and why you went into it in the first place
- Considered teaching in different types of schools or in a different role
- Started to come to terms with the situation if you have no choice about leaving the profession
- Explored how leaving teaching might affect how you feel about yourself, how others see you and the wider implications in your life
- Weighed up whether or not you're able and prepared to cope with a drop in income

That's the thinking side of things. You're probably also very aware of your gut feeling on the issue. You need to take that into account too.

It's all very well to think about what you don't want to do, but unless you have an idea of what will replace it you will probably still find it a difficult to make a decision. Part two – weighing up the options, will start to give you some ideas about what you might be able to do instead of teaching.

Part Two
Weighing up the Options

Part two looks at the different options you can explore if you want to leave teaching. Broadly speaking these can be organised into two groups:

> 1.   Careers which are not classroom teaching but are still linked to education
> 2.   Careers which are completely outside the field of education.

'When I decided to quit teaching I was on a high to start with, I thought there must be lots of other things I could do. After two weeks of job hunting I was in despair – there didn't seem to be anything an ex-teacher was qualified for. The truth was somewhere in the middle – there were opportunities but you had to look for them. A combination of patience and diligent research finally led me to my new career.'
David
Before: FE lecturer
Now: Working for the Home Office

In general, it is easier for teachers to move into education related jobs than it is to leave education altogether. The next two chapters look at both options.

Chapter Six
Staying in Education

Non-teaching jobs in schools

Some people are happy to work in schools but no longer want the responsibility of teaching. A surprising number of teachers work as teaching assistants. You sometimes hear teachers say that they can't get a job as a teaching assistant because they are overqualified but the evidence suggests that many schools are quite happy to employ qualified teachers as teaching assistants.

'I left teaching when I had my children. I knew I didn't want to return as the amount of work just wouldn't have fitted with my family life but I like working with children and I like schools so I got a job as a teaching assistant. It suits me down to the ground although occasionally I look at the teachers and think, I could do better that that! Perhaps I will teach again when my own children are older.'
Liz
Before: Primary school teacher
Now: Primary school teaching assistant

'I'm on less than half the salary I was on before but I wouldn't go back to teaching. It's just not worth the stress.'
Candy
Before: Primary school teacher

Now: Special needs secondary school teaching assistant

Following the introduction of the agreement that teachers should rarely cover for absent teachers, many schools now employ cover supervisors. This agreement is not statutory and some schools do still use teachers to provide cover but in general, cover supervisors have been found to be a cheap way of managing staff absence. You do not have to be a qualified teacher for this post and the salary is usually in line with teaching assistant pay but it is another post which some ex-teachers quite like.

'Being a cover supervisor is a bit like being a supply teacher except you know the school and a lot of the students and you feel like a member of staff. I was lucky in that my Head put me at the very top of the scale so although it's less than I would get as a teacher, I can manage on it. I still do some preparation and planning as sometimes the work I'm left is a bit 'thin', but I don't do any reports or marking and I don't have the worry of whether or not my classes are making enough progress.'
Jan
Before: History teacher
Now: Cover supervisor

There are a number of seasonal jobs if you don't need to work full time. Many schools employ temporary exam invigilators and exam boards are nearly always looking for markers.

Occasionally, ex-teachers end up working in schools but in completely different roles.

'I left teaching after only three years and retrained as an accountant. After working for a number of small firms I ended up working back in a school as a bursar.'
Lorraine
Before: Maths teacher
Now: School Bursar and Business Manager

'After leaving teaching I worked for an agency doing data entry and admin work but eventually I got a job as an exams officer and I my teaching background definitely helped me get the job.'
Georgia
Before: ICT teacher
Now: Exams officer

Private tutoring and clubs

If you still like teaching, but don't like schools, there are teaching opportunities in other settings. Private tutoring or tutoring for a private company is one of the most common routes for people leaving the classroom. It could be argued that this is not strictly leaving teaching, however it does prove to be the answer for many teachers who wish to leave the classroom. It has a number of advantages over other jobs:

- You are already fully qualified to do it
- In most areas there is a fair amount of work
- You can charge a higher hourly rate than you would get in many other jobs
- You are your own boss (unless you work for another organisation)
- You get to do the part of the job you still love i.e. teaching, without any of the paperwork, politics, scrutiny or other aspects of teaching you might not like
- You can keep up to date with teaching and will probably find it easier to return to classroom teaching if you decide to at a later date

Tutoring does have a few disadvantages:

- It is almost always part time
- Some teachers find one to one teaching boring
- Unless you work for a company you will have to use your own home or travel to the pupils' homes
- You may feel isolated

A few tutors have found ways to make tutoring full time or almost full time.

'I have a number of private pupils who I tutor in the evenings and at weekends. There is a high demand for eleven plus tutoring in my area. This gave me quite a good income but none of it is during the day. This year I have found some day work too. One of my local schools employs me using pupil premium money to do one to one literacy and numeracy work. I have also contacted social services and from time to time they have looked after children who have been excluded from school or who are refusing to attend school. They pay me to tutor the children in their home or foster placements until they can attend school again.'
Davina
Before: English and history teacher
Now: Private tutor

'I give private music lessons. I have some adult clients who have lessons during the day and a large number of school age children in the evenings. I also teach four different music groups during the day. One is for a group of home schooled pupils, one is at a primary school where they don't have a music teacher, one is in a day centre for adults with learning difficulties and the other is a sing along session in a care home for elderly people. I really love the group work, it's so varied but always good fun.'

Chris
Before: Music teacher
Now: Private tutor

In recent years there has been an explosion of after school educational provision and you may well find that one of the national tutoring groups suits you very well. You will not have the hassle of finding your own pupils and there is a certain amount of support in terms of training and resources. Some ex-teachers have chosen to pioneer their own after school provision.

'As well as private tutoring I run after school language clubs in three different primary schools. There is always a waiting list for places.'
Alison
Before: Teacher of modern foreign languages
Now: Private tutor

Other successful after school clubs include cooking, gardening, art, drama and dance.
As well as after school clubs there are the stage schools which offer holiday and weekend courses. There are a number of groups offering dance, drama and singing clubs. Some of these employ staff directly and others run as franchises. If there is already one in your area then you may find there isn't enough demand for another one but if not and you have the relevant experience it could be worth considering.

You may find opportunities in post 16 training. All young people up to the age of 18 have to be engaged in some form of education or training now. This has led to an expansion in apprenticeships and courses offering vocational training. In general NVQ assessors come from within the industry in which they are assessing rather than a teaching background, but there are exceptions.

'I work for a training company as a trainer and NVQ assessor. Most of the young people I work with need help with their literacy and numeracy and that's really what I specialise in.'
Anna
Was: Primary school teacher
Now: NVQ trainer an assessor

'I left teaching after only a year and worked in retail for about five years. I was approached by the company I worked for to see if I wanted to get involved in their training scheme because my manager knew I had been a teacher. Now I'm a full time NVQ trainer and assessor. I used to think the time I spent doing my teacher training was wasted but it's funny how things work out.'
Wendy
Was: RE teacher
Now: NVQ assessor and trainer

Teaching the teachers

Educational consultancy is another area that has boomed in recent years. Once upon a time local education authorities employed thousands of advisers. Whilst some of these were highly thought of, there was sometimes a feeling that advisory posts were a good way to pension off senior teachers who could no longer hack it in the classroom. Whatever the truth of the matter, many of these posts have now gone and authorities have far fewer advisory posts on offer. Much of their work has been taken over by private consultancy firms or by educational charitable trusts.

Consultancy work can be a well paid opportunity for ex-teachers but you need to have a very strong career background where you can show that you have been successful at leading a team, implementing change and raising standards. Schools who pay individuals or companies for consultancy work or in-service training expect to get measurable improvements in terms of exam, national curriculum and Ofsted grades as a direct result of their input. Many successful consultants have a particular expertise.

'I was a primary school teacher for ten years. During that time I found that using IT in a really dynamic way could motivate the children like nothing else. Children are natural IT specialists – it's part of their world. Now I work as a consultant and I see the same enthusiasm in the

teachers I teacher as I used to in the children. It's great to think they'll be passing that on in the classroom.'
Nick
Before: Primary KS leader
Now: Educational consultant

If you still have plenty of enthusiasm and energy for teaching, a wealth of good ideas and are looking for a new challenge then consultancy work may well be worth considering.

Many experienced teachers have been involved in training student teachers in some form. You may have been a mentor or had a student teacher in your department. From time to time posts come up for teacher trainers in Universities or other organisations and this can be a very satisfying way of leaving classroom teaching but continuing to use all your teaching skills.

'I lecture in Teacher Training. I loved teaching and I was an Advanced Skills Teacher but after 15 years I felt it was time for a change. I'd been involved in school in various teacher training programmes so when a vacancy came up at a nearby university I went for it.'
Linda
Was: Advanced Skills Teacher in RE and PSHCE
Now: Lecturer in Teacher Training

Teaching adults

Most towns have a range of adult education classes which are taught by qualified teachers. These range from basic English and maths, through creative classes such as pottery or print making right up to 'A' level classes. Many are evening courses. You may be required to take an adult education qualification but this can usually be taken once you have started. In recent years there has been a growth in literacy, numeracy and ICT courses, especially where these are linked to improving employment prospects. In contrast the number of creative and recreational courses seems to have gone down owing to repeated rounds of local authority budget cuts. Luckily, many businesses are increasing the amount of training they offer their employees and there are now full time jobs to be found in these areas. Often these jobs are occupied by former teachers.

'I do first aid training for a charity. We have a large contract with the local authority but also train up first aiders for private businesses. Some of our courses are Ofqual accredited and teaching has to be of a high standard.'
Helena
Before: PE teacher
Now: First Aid instructor

'I work for a large business delivering IT training to our employees. I'm responsible for

identifying the training needs, putting together the courses and delivering the training.'
Gordon
Before: Sixth form maths teacher
Now: IT trainer

Educational publishing
As a teacher you have probably spent many hours preparing resources and if you're the sort of person whose resources are often borrowed by other people you may wonder whether or not you could make a living out of this. It is definitely a field which is occupied by ex-teachers as it is very difficult to produce resources without the experience of teaching.

Fortunately for teachers, but unfortunately for those wishing to make money out of resources, there are a number of sites which offer free teaching resources, designed by teachers, and this has made it more difficult for teachers to make money out of writing resources. The TES website has over 800,000 free resources, many of which are of excellent quality. Other sites, for example Teachit, do pay their contributors royalties. As a teacher, you are probably producing resources anyway, so putting them on Teachit with the chance of earning something makes sense but most of their contributors make very little. As a guideline they advise that '10 resources (averaging around three pages per resources) on Teachit are currently earning around £60 a year.'

A few prolific contributors do make considerably more than this, but for most, it is simply a way of making a little extra while they teach and having the satisfaction of knowing their resources are appreciated.

Nevertheless, educational writing can be lucrative.

'I worked part time initially, but now work full time writing educational resources, mostly text books but also content for websites. Each curriculum change offers new opportunities either to update or write something new.'
Sharon
Before: English and special needs teacher
Now: Educational writer

A number of large educational and children's book publishers still use reps to visit schools and sell their resources and this is another job which is popular with ex-teachers. It can be a very flexible career which is mostly carried out during term time. The earnings are usually on a commission basis but if you can build up a good number of schools you can make a reasonable amount. Many reps also host book selling parties in people's homes or hold a stall at local fairs. It's probably true to say that most book reps use it as a way of earning extra income to supplement their partner's earnings, but it's not impossible to build your business up to the point where it becomes your main income. Some publishers have a system where you become a team leader which means that you derive an income from the work done by others in your team.

'I stopped teaching when my daughter was born and started selling children's books when she was about three. To begin with it was just a way of keeping my brain going and earning a little bit of money on the side but when my husband was made redundant I went all out and found I could make a decent amount of money. I may go back to teaching one day, but at the minute I'm really enjoying being my own boss. I'm not a natural sales person but I really love these books and I think people can tell my enthusiasm is genuine.'
Natalie
Before: Geography teacher
Now: Book rep

A huge advantage of this job is that in most cases you don't have to wait for a vacancy to come up. You can simply contact the publishers and begin. You would do well to find out how many reps are already in your area though, in case the market is already at saturation point.

Education in other settings
Hospital teaching is often suggested as a good alternative to classroom teaching but this is not always as straight forward as it seems. In many authorities hospital teaching is attached to other

'out of school' cases and whilst you may find you are simply visiting sick children you may also be required to teach children with challenging behaviour who have been excluded or are unable to attend school for other reasons. This may be a job you love but be sure to find out exactly what sort of referrals the organisation takes before you apply for work.

Many charities and organisations employ ex-teachers to deliver some of the educational parts of their service. These can be fantastic jobs as they often involve working with groups of children who arrive with their teachers. You get to do the teaching but, by and large, they will deal with the behaviour management. These jobs tend to come up infrequently and there are often large numbers of applicants. There are ways of increasing your chances at landing one of these sought after posts and we will be looking at this in a later chapter. The types of organisations that use this sort of approach include charities, museums, art galleries, science parks and outdoor education facilities.

'I work in a Science Centre. We run sessions for school groups here at the centre and we also go into schools. I run some of the groups, produce resources for teachers to use in school and sometimes advise on the exhibitions as well. I really love the workshops – I get to teach without all the other stuff that isn't teaching that teachers have to do. You do have to be able to

manage big groups though, and you have to think on your feet because you don't know the group and sometimes, if it's not going too well, you have to be able to adapt. It's crucial that you keep them interested and the teachers feel it's worthwhile because we rely on schools rebooking year after year.'
Khalid
Before: Science teacher
Now: Education team member at Science Centre

'I work for an environmental charity. We run outdoor day or half day sessions for schools doing practical activities. There are only five of us in the team and between us we plan, prepare and deliver all the sessions. It involves a lot of behind the scenes work such as thinking up new projects and researching areas of the curriculum that we can link to. The workshops we run are really only the final element of the job. We take children of all ages and we also do quite a bit of special education teaching. I might be working with a group of primary aged children with severe learning difficulties in the morning and a group of disaffected teenagers who've been excluded from school in the afternoon. You have to be able to relate to all of them and switch gear quickly.'
Emma
Before: Middle school teacher
Now: Field Instructor for environmental charity

'I'm part of the education team at a museum. In fact we cover three museums in the area. We run sessions and loan items to schools as well as providing resources. My job is pretty varied, sometimes I run sessions for school visits but I also attend local country fairs, we run summer drop in sessions in local libraries and we've just started offering teacher training sessions too.'
Lara
Before: Humanities teacher
Now: Museum education officer

Non-teaching jobs within education
We have already looked at consultancy work. There are a few other areas of education where ex-teachers have an advantage. Some of these may be available as secondments rather than permanent jobs.

'I'm an educational welfare officer. I love the job and it really helps having been a teacher as it means you understand the system well. The job has got harder though; we have four less people in the team now than when I started but we get more referrals. I do sometimes feel I'm not doing everything I should which is how I often felt when I was teaching.'
Julie
Was: Assistant Head of Year
Now: Educational Welfare Officer

'I was an ICT teacher but I moved to a prison and worked as an instructor there for a while. Then I got a job in the same prison as a Learning and Skills Adviser. I don't teach now, instead I do one to one interviews where we look at their needs and plan things like courses, literacy or numeracy support and work placements. I also work with the prison officers to help set targets for the inmates, liaise with other agencies and organise courses.'
Carolyn
Before: ICT teacher
Now: Learning and Skill Adviser in a prison

Most ex-teachers, particularly those who have taught for a few years, move into careers that are linked to education in some way. Although they are still likely to take a pay cut, moving into a job which requires some kind of teaching background can mean the reduction is less than if you are starting from scratch.

Exercise ten
Getting an overview of possible opportunities
Skim read the examples of ex-teachers quoted in this chapter and jot down any career paths you think might interest you. Do a google job search to see if those kind of opportunities might be available in your area. On many job sites you can tick a box so that your search only includes jobs currently available. If you unclick the box you will

see all the jobs that have come up in the past. This will give you an overview of the types of opportunities around which might come up again in the future.

Chapter Seven
Leaving Education Completely

Dream jobs

As a teacher, you will have heard the old joke 'Those who can, do, those who can't, teach.' It's usually used as an insult and whilst it falls very far of the mark, there may be a grain of truth in it. Most secondary schools contain an art teacher who would really like to be an artist, an English teacher who wants to write, a drama teacher who wants to act, or a PE teacher who never quite made it into professional football. Perhaps you secretly harbour a dream that you feel is unrealistic and have settled for teaching instead. Your dream may not be about being rich or famous. You may have wanted to be a chef but knew the hours were completely unsociable so settled for teaching Home Economics instead.

If, deep down, you know what you want to do, but think it is just a pipe dream, just remember, many celebrities who are now house hold names started out as teachers. A number of famous authors were previously teachers. Michael Morpurgo was a Primary School teacher, Philip Pullman taught in a Middle School and Joanne Harris taught modern foreign languages. If you browse through publishers' websites and look at the biographies of their authors you will find a number of ex-teachers. It is less common in other artistic fields but you can find ex-teachers in many areas. Former teachers turned musicians include Sting and Sheryl Crow, teachers turned comedians include former Geography teacher Rob Rouse and ex-science teacher Shazia Mirza. Actors who were once teachers include Brendon Gleeson and artists include former Head of Art Michael Worobec.

These former teachers are evidence that it is possible to move from teaching into a full time career as a performer, writer or artist, but the majority of them did not give up teaching, or another full time day job, until they had already begun to experience some kind of success in their chosen field. You may feel that teaching is preventing you from succeeding elsewhere, because it leaves you no time to work at other things. There are a number of ways to look at this. If you really want to write, you could find time, the question is, how badly do you want to succeed and what else are you prepared to give up to put in the effort required? Could you teach part time, or can you afford to take a year out, with the promise that if after a year you are no nearer to achieving your dream, you could return to teaching?

Following your dream may be a risk and you will have to weigh it up against your responsibilities. Don't dismiss it altogether though. Look at all the possibilities and see whether or not you can find a way to give yourself that chance.

Training for a new career

If you have decided to leave education all together, and you are still in the position where you want to be earning a decent wage or move up the career ladder you may have to consider retraining. This can be a difficult decision to make if you have already spent four years or more earning a degree and teacher training qualification. Some examples of routes taken by ex-teachers are given below.

Nursing: minimum three years. If you have a degree in Biology you may be able to shorten it a little.

Social work: Three year undergraduate degree or two year MA. Most providers will require you to have around six months experience of social care.

'I worked in a residential school organising work experience and giving careers advice for children with emotional and behavioural difficulties. I then got a job as a social care assistant with the local authority. They sponsored me to do a degree to become a qualified social worker. They paid me my fees and a small wage while I studied. I couldn't have afforded it if I'd had to pay for the course myself.'
Marnie
Before: Careers adviser in residential school
Now: Qualified social worker

Book keeping and Accountancy: There are a range of accountancy qualifications from book keeping right through to Chartered and Certified Accountants. There are many distance learning courses which can be taken part time. It is a fairly popular route for ex-teachers.

'I started doing the books for my husband's plumbing business on an informal basis and found I liked it so I took an Open University Certificate in Accounting. After that I took an AAT level 3 diploma in accounting at which point I gave up teaching as I was able to get plenty of work with small businesses doing their accounts and helping them with their tax returns. I would like to become a full chartered accountant in the future.'
Lianne
Before: Music teacher
Now: Book keeping and basic accounts

Psychotherapy and Counselling: In order to register as a counsellor with the British Association for Counselling and Psychotherapy (BACP) you would need to undertake a Diploma that is classroom based and includes a minimum of a 100 hours supervised placement. These courses are typically a year full time or two or more years part time. Although there are many on-line courses advertised for counselling, the BACP recommend these only as introductions as they are not usually able to offer the 100 hours supervised practice. Training to become a full psychotherapist usually takes four years or more. Some health authorities offer training schemes.

'I taught for 20 years before training as a counsellor and then as a psychotherapist, hypnotherapist and child psychologist. I've spent the last 20 years developing and delivering training to professionals in the UK and Europe as well as having a busy private practice of my own. I wish I'd left teaching much sooner.'
Lorie
Before: Science teacher
Now: Psychotherapist, supervisor and trainer

Using you subject skills
As a subject specialist you may find there is a natural fit for new work. English teachers may find work proof reading, editing, copywriting or in journalism.

'Initially I found work proofreading, and from that I moved into editing. At the same time I used some on-line freelance sites to get writing work. To begin with it was horribly badly paid, but as I built up my portfolio I was gradually able to charge more and more. I also approached local magazines and pitched ideas for articles. It took me a long time to break into the industry but I now write regularly for two magazines and do one off pieces for a number of others.'
Gary

Before: English teacher
Now: Freelance writer and editor

Language teachers should make the most of their skills too.

'I started off using an on-line freelance site to get translation work. Through that I got regular work with two companies and then I was offered a full time job by one of them.'
Marcus
Before: Head of Modern Foreign Languages department
Now: Company translator

Art teachers might want to think about graphic design, ICT teachers could look at programming and software development, scientists might look at lab technician work. If you are a secondary school teacher you probably have a subject degree which might lead you into a specific direction. Think back to when you graduated. What line of work did your fellow graduates move into? Carry out a bit of research on social media sites to find out what they're all doing now.

Don't want a new career, just a job?
You may not be looking for a new career. You may simply want a job that will pay the bills and which doesn't involve Ofsted or marking. In that case, if you are prepared to start at the bottom, you could apply for almost any position.

However, there are a few industries that seem more of a natural fit for ex-teachers. Any of these could develop into a career you may not even have thought of.

Anything sales related and jobs in marketing may well use skills you have in abundance. You are used to speaking to an audience, 'selling' you subject, projecting enthusiasm. You are also adept at meeting deadlines, working under pressure and hitting targets.

Human resources work will tap into your 'people skills'. It also involves a fair amount of analytical work, as you would be working with policies, procedures and regulations. Your experience of deciphering exam specifications and using performance management tools can all be presented as relevant experience.

Other areas ex-teachers have successfully found work in include events planning, retail, charity fund raising, customer services, administration, estate agency, reception and construction.

Working for yourself

Starting your own business can be risky, but there are ways of minimising the risk. You may well have a talent or idea which you think you could turn into a profit making endeavour. There are lots of websites and books offering advice for new businesses, and there is no doubt that many ex-teachers have become self-employed very successfully as the following examples show.

'I used to get really annoyed at my local gym listening to some of the personal trainers there. They seemed to do the same stuff with everyone and some of them just didn't seem to care. I was sure I could do a better job. I took on a few private clients through word of mouth and I soon found myself working four or five nights a week. I felt a bit of a fraud as I wasn't qualified so I took an on-line course and after that it was an easy decision to give up teaching and do personal training full time. I've linked up with a friend who is a nutritionist and we now offer a twelve week new-lifestyle programme. It's been really popular.'
John
Before: PE teacher
Now: Personal trainer

'I became quite ill from teaching and had to quit. I started doing a bit of gardening and some odd jobs just to get me out of the house. Within a couple of months I was working full time. I live by the coast and in the spring I get a lot of work painting beach huts. It's fairly lucrative and I've never been so healthy in my life.'
Simon
Before: Senior teacher and maths teacher
Now: Handyman and gardener

'After my children were born I knew I didn't want to go back to teaching. I'd had some back problems and my health visitor advised me to try yoga. I was hooked from the first session and I just wanted to know more and more. Learning to teach yoga seemed like a natural progression. I now run about four groups a week as well as doing some short courses. It's not a full time job but it makes a significant contribution to our income.'
Vicki
Before: Primary teacher
Now: Yoga teacher

'I run a complimentary therapy business specialising in reflexology and aromatherapy. Most of my clients are private and I work in their own homes but I also have a few sessions at a nearby health spa. I love being my own boss and I've never had an unsatisfied client so the job satisfaction is amazing.'
Nina
Before: Geography teacher
Now: Complimentary therapist

'I started selling my old clothes through ebay, and then I found I had a bit of a knack for wording things and photographing them so I started selling things for friends too. Now I have a fulltime business managing an on-line vintage clothing shop. I think my shop was one of the first but since I started out lots more vintage on-

line shops have started up too so I don't know how long I'll carry on being successful.'
Karen
Before: Technology teacher
Now: On-line vintage clothing business

'My partner started up a wedding planning business not long after we got married. Within months she had more work than she could handle so I (gratefully!) gave up my job and now I work with her.'
Darren
Before: History and RE teacher
Now: Assistant wedding planner

Buying into a Franchise

If you don't have an idea for a successful business, but you'd still like to be your own boss, you could buy into a franchise. This would be your own business but you'd have the back up of a larger company. Franchises vary enormously in how much support they offer but they usually include basic training, products, some administrative support and publicity.

Before jumping in there are a number of questions you need to ask yourself.

- How much money do I want to invest?
- How many hours am I prepared to work?

- How quickly do I need to make a profit?
- How much risk am I prepared to take?
- How much space will the business need?
- What am I good at?
- How much stress can I handle?

The franchise business has grown enormously in the last twenty years and there are around 930 franchise brands operating in the UK with 39,000 outlets. The good news is that 92% of these report a profit. The bad news is that there are an overwhelming number of websites and consultancies offering advice, and it is difficult to know which ones are the most reputable. The best place to start is at the British Franchise Association website. This association is a voluntary, self-regulatory body and members have to meet certain standards to join. They provide an enormous amount of information which includes step by step guidance on choosing a franchise.

There are too many franchises to list but franchises which have been successfully run by ex-teachers include franchises in Premier Sports, Mail Boxes Etc, Pyjama Drama, Tumble Tots, Tutor Doctor and Cash Generator. Inevitably many ex-teachers choose education or child related franchises, but there is a vast range of other areas and as long as you have the skills there is nothing to stop you moving into a completely different type of work. The British Franchise Association lists over forty franchise categories ranging from familiar ones such as health and beauty services and pet care to some you may not have thought of including property management and Christmas Decorators .

Exercise eleven
What are you going to do?
Are you ready to make a decision? This chapter has looked at a number of options and sooner or later you need to decide which direction you're going in. Essentially you need to make a choice about whether you want to stay in education in some form or do something completely different. Once you've made that decision you can either:

- Retrain
- Look for a job
- Start your own independent or franchised business.

Go back to the sections which interest you most and think through the possibilities. Sleep on it for a while and discuss it with those people it might affect or people you think might give you good advice. Look back at the figures you generated at the end of chapter six and start to think about whether the ideas you're moving towards could generate the amount of money you estimate you'll need.

Remember to pay attention to your gut feelings. Is there one particular idea that gets you more excited than anything else? Is there an idea you keep coming back to, although on the surface it seems ridiculous? Hopefully, sooner or later you'll have a clear idea of what you want to do. Once you have that, you can begin to plan.

Part Three
Making it Happen

Part three assumes you've made the decision to leave teaching and looks at the practical steps you need to take next. By the end of this section you should have a clear idea of where you're going, how long it will take and what your need to do to make it happen.

'Leaving teaching was a very easy decision, what to do next was reasonably easy, but how to make it happen was much harder. I knew I couldn't leave until I'd got my business off the ground but I couldn't get my business of the ground while I was still teaching. With hindsight I realise I needed a much clearer plan and a more realistic time scale. I wasted a lot of time and effort doing things in the wrong order or missing opportunities because I hadn't thought ahead. For example, I put out adverts just before my students were due to finish their coursework. I suddenly had a load of enquiries for my new business at the same time as having to mark dozens of coursework folders.'
Peter
Before: English teacher
Now: Website designer

Chapter Eight
Job Hunting

Before we move on here's a piece of advice. You may be getting quite excited now about the thought of leaving teaching. The advice is, don't tell anyone at work yet. There may be a gap of some time between making the decision to leave and actually leaving. Apart from the usual period of notice, you may need time to sort out finances or to put other plans in place. People's attitudes towards you can change once they think you are leaving. They may consider that your 'heart isn't in the job' anymore, and start finding fault with what you do. You may encounter resentment from others who would like to leave but feel they can't. Because teachers have to give long notice periods we are often in the position of working alongside colleagues who will be leaving in three or even four months' time. You may have been on the end of comments yourself in the past where you were moving to a new job and found that people began to sideline you or make snide remarks about you not caring.

'I was really excited about my new career but looking back, I think it annoyed people and I should have spoken about it less. I probably came across as a bit smug.'
Alex
Before: Art teacher

Now: Art therapist

Skills audit and CV
Your first planning task is to carry out a full skills audit. This is important whether you plan to retrain, apply for jobs or start you own business. Any job or course application you submit will need a clear sighted assessment of your skills, and any business plan you need to write should bear your skills in mind too.

Go back to the list you wrote in exercise two of all the things you do in your current job. For each task note down the skills you use to carry out that task. Be as detailed as possible, for example, marking includes the skills of paying attention to detail, ability to evaluate, interpretation of success criteria, ability to encourage and give positive feedback and the ability to meet tight deadlines. Try to identify the skills you consider yourself to be particularly good at.

Once you've worked thought the list, add any other skills you may have evidence for from other areas in your life. Think about the qualities you feel you have too, for example honesty, compassion, enthusiasm or tolerance. If you're short of ideas a quick internet search for 'personal qualities' will give you lists to choose from.

Your next task is to write your CV. Again, the internet will show you how to lay it out if you're unsure. It should include basic personal details (name, address), your education and qualifications, an employment history and a brief personal statement. It is well worth writing a CV even if you don't plan to apply for job or if all the applications you've seen are on line. Having all the information at your fingertips can save hours in constantly trying to find it again each time you fill out an application and you never know when a chance conversation might lead to a request for your CV. Job applications are hugely time consuming but they are much quicker if you have a CV and a skills audit sitting next to you.

Searching for jobs

By now you should have a good idea of the type of work you are looking for, and this will dictate where you need to look. If your new career or job is to be education based then the Times Education Supplement is still the best starting point (either the paper or their website.) The Guardian is also worth looking at. Local Education Authorities all have their own websites where jobs are advertised and with some of these you can upload your details as well as signing up for job alerts. If you are looking for work in the independent sector the Independent Schools Council and the Independent Association of Prep Schools have useful sites. They don't advertise jobs but they will give you information about all the independent schools in your area.

For non-education jobs the choice can be bewildering. The following websites are frequently listed as among the best job listing websites in the uk:

- jobseekers.direct.gov.uk (the government job website.)
- reed.co.uk (an employment agency. Look for a branch in your area as well as their comprehensive website.)
- monster.co.uk
- indeed.co.uk
- everyjobsite.co.uk
- jobsite.co.uk
- fish4.co.uk

For jobs with specific organisations the following sites are useful:

- NHS jobs are advertised at www.jobs.nhs.uk as well as on individual health authority websites
- Civil service jobs are at www.civilservicejobs.service.gov.uk
- Prison service jobs can be found by following the links at nomsjobs.com. (noms stands for National Offender Management Services)
- The two main sites for jobs in the charity sector are

www.charityjob.co.uk and
jobs.thirdsector.co.uk

Don't forget your local paper, and do be proactive
about asking around, especially if you know
people working in the sector you're interested in.

Employment issues which are specific to ex-teachers

There are plenty of websites and books available
where you can find advice on applying for jobs
and interview techniques and there seems little
point covering those areas here. However, there
are a number of issues specific to would be ex-
teachers which you need to think through
carefully.

Why do you want to leave teaching?
This question may come up in a formal interview
and could come in a number of guises e.g. 'Why
do you want to leave your current job?'

As a teacher, it would be easy to launch
into a list of grievances about the teaching
profession but this is a mistake. As soon as you
touch on the unreasonable hours, myriad causes
of stress, unrealistic expectations or any of the
other negatives you may be aware of, you run the
risk of giving out three equally destructive
messages. In the first place, you will sound like a
very negative person who likes to moan, and
nobody wants to employ one of those. Secondly,
you may come across as someone who is just

trying to escape from teaching. Your new would-be employer wants to hear that you want to work for them, not that you are just looking for a way out of teaching. Thirdly, you run the risk of implying that the job you are applying for is easier than teaching. This is likely to make you sound arrogant and could suggest that you don't appreciate the complexity of the new job or the dedication and effort required to succeed in it.

The best line to take if you have taught for a while is that you have very much enjoyed teaching but you feel it's time for a new challenge. If you haven't been teaching long then take the line that, while you've found it interesting, you've realised that it's not what you want to be doing for the rest of your life. Ideally you need to convert the question into why you really, really want the new job. You need to show that you are looking forward, not running away (even if you secretly feel otherwise).

Your skills and experiences
Teaching today covers a huge variety of skills and, whilst this is a huge strength, you do need to be realistic about what you've actually done. You will have heard people say that as a teacher you are expected to be a social worker, secretary, entertainer and surrogate parent as well as a teacher. Don't make the mistake of believing this as once again this can show a real lack of understanding of the job you are applying for. You do not have experience of social work,

however much you may feel you have done over and above your role as a teacher. If asked how you think you'd cope in a particular situation by all means compare it to something you have done but acknowledge the differences.

'When I was being interviewed for the post of Community Support Officer with the police I was asked how I would cope if faced with a group of men fighting outside a pub. I was tempted to say, 'I've handled 9B on a Friday afternoon so I think I'd cope,' but I knew that would be stupid. Instead I talked about the time I had to intervene between two teenagers arguing in the playground. I said that I realised it wasn't the same thing but I described how I had been aware of my adrenalin rising and I knew my first priority was to keep myself safe, get help, and try to keep everyone else safe. I said that I'd managed to keep very calm so I thought that showed that I could think clearly under pressure.'
Billy
Before: PE teacher
Now: Community Support Officer

How would you cope without the school holidays? This comes up surprisingly often, generally not in the formal interview but during conversation whist being shown around or during informal chats. Don't say you work most of the holidays anyway; no none-teacher believes that. Try to play it down by saying you prefer the flexibility of choosing when you can go on holiday or simply say it doesn't bother you.

How do you feel about taking a pay cut or a reduction in status?
If you have taught for a while, and particularly if you have been in a senior position, prospective employers can be a little suspicious of your reasons for wanting to step down. You don't want to give the impression that you are tired and are just looking for an easier life. You can talk about how learning a new job will be a challenge in itself, explain that you are happy to start at the bottom so that you can learn all about this new career, or say that you hope to progress quite quickly so that you are in a senior position again before too long.

Think about the most appropriate answer for the job you are applying for and avoid coming across as someone who is hugely relieved to be giving up responsibility. Of course, this may not apply if you are going for a job as a shelf stacker in your local supermarket in which case you might want to be more up front about the fact that you are perfectly willing and able to work hard, but that you are looking for a job without any major responsibility for managing other people.

When would you be available to start?

Most jobs require people to give a month's notice. Teaching can be anything from six weeks to seven months depending on the time of year. In most state and many independent schools, if you haven't handed your notice in by the 31st May, you are committed to staying until the end of December. That's seven months. Clearly, very few employers are going to be prepared to wait that long for you to take up a post. You have three choices.

You could hand your notice in before you have secured a job, and simply hope that you get something. Unless you can afford to be out of work this is probably not a good idea. Even if you can afford it, being out of work can sometimes make it more difficult to get a job, as employers can be suspicious of career breaks unless you have a clear reason, such as child care, to explain it.

Your second option is to speak to your Head and try to negotiate an earlier exit. Many Heads will be willing to accommodate this, particularly if they know you are leaving teaching. Your best bet is probably to wait until you have been offered a job before beginning to negotiate. If you approach your Head speculatively and they say no which could put you in a difficult position. If you already have a job offer there is more pressure on the Head to agree as otherwise they could be responsible for your having the job offer withdrawn. You will probably already have had to ask for time off for an interview so it shouldn't come as a complete surprise to them.

Lastly, if you are offered a job and the Head and chair of governors refuse to release you early you have a difficult decision to make. You could choose to break your contract. If you do this your employer is entitled to recoup any expenses incurred as a result of your leaving early and this, in theory, could be the cost of recruiting and paying a supply teacher to cover your remaining notice period minus whatever they would have paid you. I am not aware of any authority ever having done this but they are legally entitled to. A much more likely consequence is that it would affect your reference, or the Head could refuse to write you a reference at all. Bear in mind the fact that many jobs ask for references from your two previous jobs, so this might affect you in the future. You will have to balance this risk against the possibility of losing out on a job you want. It is best to negotiate an early exit if at all possible.

If you are asked by a prospective employer about when you would be able to start you should explain what your normal notice period would be but say that you believe the Head might be willing to negotiate an earlier exit.

Starting your own business

If you are planning on selling a product or providing a service then you are starting your own business and you need to be business-like from the very beginning. It's quite common for people to start with a hobby which gradually grows until they suddenly realise that they're earning money and need to be thinking about paying tax and keeping records. Any earnings you make have to be declared, even if they fall below your personal tax allowance. Keeping accurate records from the start will also mean that you can claim allowable expenses as you will have the receipts required to do so. If you decide to employ an accountant or bookkeeper, you should still make sure you keep a written record of everything you spend and earn and keep any receipts. You will probably be paying your accountant by the hour so the easier you make it for them the cheaper it will be for you.

If you plan to borrow money to start your business you will need a business plan. Even if you don't plan to borrow, a clear business plan will improve your chances of success and will make it easier for you to access suitable training or advice.

As always, there is an overwhelming amount of advice on the internet. The best place to start is with the government websites:

- https://www.gov.uk/starting-up-a-business
- http://www.hmrc.gov.uk/startingup (Her Majesties Revenue and Customs website)

- http://business.scotland.gov.uk/to pic/starting-up-a-business (For advice relating to Scotland)
- http://business.wales.gov.uk/starti ng-business (For Wales)

From these you will also find links on record keeping, registering as self-employed, national insurance information and managing your tax affairs, including information on allowable expenses.

Most banks offer advice, although of course this is not always impartial. Smallbusiness.co.uk is also a useful site with a large number of high quality articles but once again, bear in mind that this website is a profit making website which relies on advertising.

Exercise 12
Skills audit and CV

If you haven't done so already, carry out a skills audit and write your CV. It really will save you time when you are applying for jobs.

Chapter Nine
Managing the Transition

The journey from teacher to a new career is often not straight forward. The two case studies below are fairly typical in that each of the teachers interviewed spent several years building up their new careers. In both cases compromises had to be made along the way.

Case study one
Teacher to full time writer
Clare taught English in comprehensive for four years, then worked for a further four years in a pupil referral unit. She then decided that she wanted a break from teaching as she was finding it difficult to manage a full time job along with raising two young children of her own. Child care costs were also a factor in her decision to give up work. She and her husband had managed to save enough so that they could manage for about a year before she would need to work again.

Clare saw a flyer from a company that produced photocopiable materials for schools who were looking to recruit new writers. She sent off some worksheets she had written and was invited to attend a day's training. She was taken on by the company as a part time writer. The job required her to interview teachers, then translate their ideas into a pack of worksheets in the house style of the company. Each pack took between four to six days to write. At first the work was sporadic and she only wrote four packs in the first six months. She was paid a flat fee and it worked out at about the same rate as supply teaching. After a while she was given more work until she was writing about two packs a month. This generated enough income for her to manage on so she didn't have to return to teaching once her savings had gone.

Through this company she met an editor who had an idea for a series of text books. Together they wrote a proposal, approached a different publishing company and pitched the idea. The series was commissioned and over the next year they researched and wrote the series. In the meantime Clare began to use online sites like elance to find other work. At first this earned very little but gradually, as she built up her reputation, she was able to charge more and companies came back to her for repeat work. She specialised in education and wrote worksheets, curriculum guides and web site content. At this point the original company folded and her income dropped significantly. She did some private tutoring and some consultancy work for a local school helping them write some of their curriculum documents.

The series of text books turned out to be very successful and Clare received regular royalties from this over the next five years. She was commissioned to write a series of other books for the same company, and after five years she was asked to update the original series which then boosted sales. By now she was also writing for local magazines as well as having a steady stream of work from contacts made through the internet.

Clare now works full time as a writer earning about the same as a classroom teacher.

Case study two
PE teacher to Psychotherapist
Craig was a PE teacher, then a head of year, then a deputy head. He increasingly felt that schools were becoming factories where creativity and individualism was stifled. The Head teacher became ill and Craig was asked to be acting Head while they advertised and appointed a new one. He had a number of disagreements with the governing body and became more and more disillusioned. The stress began to make him ill. When they appointed a new Headteacher Craig resigned and asked that they allow him to leave without serving his notice. The governors agreed and Craig left more or less overnight.

Craig had been separated from his wife for two years and in the same month that he resigned his divorce was finalised. The family house was sold and Craig was able to live on the proceeds for a few months. He had taken a counselling course several years earlier and now decided that he would like to train as a psychotherapist. Although he did not want to return to teaching, he could not afford to train without earning. He applied for a job at a school for children with emotional and behavioural difficulties. He didn't get the job but asked the Head if he could do some voluntary work there. After working as a volunteer for half a term, one of the teachers went on maternity leave and Craig was taken on to cover her for two terms. At the end of this a permanent vacancy arose which Craig applied for and this time he was appointed.

He carried on working at the EBD school while continuing with his psychotherapy training. The Head was very supportive and granted Craig unpaid leave on a number of occasions so that he could attend conferences and training events. Working at this school renewed Craig's faith in teaching as he felt it was much more child centred, however he was determined to pursue a career in psychotherapy and after three years moved to a 0.6 contract. This enabled him to begin to build up his own therapy business.

By now, Craig had a new partner who lived in a different part of the country. Craig made the decision to move so that he could live with his new partner. He worked part time as an instructor in a young offenders' institute while finishing his training and building up his therapy business from scratch again. After two years he was able to resign from the instructor's job.

Craig now works full time as a psychotherapist.

Compromise and building up the new career

Neither of the teachers above moved immediately from teaching to another full time job. Both had to rely on savings while they built up their new careers, and both had to return to teaching in some form or other to supplement their earnings before they were in a position to leave teaching altogether. This is not unusual, especially where the new career includes an element of training.

You may feel that you simply do not have the time or the energy to establish a new career while you are still teaching but quitting your job completely in the hope that you are going to be successful may turn out to be more stressful than teaching, especially if you have a family to support. There are a few alternatives.

Think about setting a date in the future when you will leave teaching and then work out how much you can save up so that you have a buffer for a few months.

'I'd always joked about going to work in Tesco and I was mortified when I applied and didn't even get an interview. I phoned the recruitment team and they were very honest with me. They said that it was partly because they didn't believe I would stick with it and partly because I had no retail experience. It was a real kick in the teeth. I carried on teaching for another year but during that year I saved every penny I could. By the end I had managed to save almost three month's

wages. I left the school in July and immediately volunteered at a local charity shop. After eight weeks a job came up as manager of another charity shop in the town. I applied and got it. I worked there for two years before moving to my current job. In the end I hardly used my savings but I needed the security to be able to leave my job.'

Judith

Before: Primary school teacher

Now: Manager of high street health food shop

Another way to transition from teaching to something else is to reduce your hours.

'When I started (selling second-hand clothes online) I was still teaching full time. I wanted to make it a full time business but several people, including my partner, didn't think it would work. A colleague of mine wanted to return to work part time after her maternity leave and the Head agreed to us doing a job share. For the next two terms I taught for two and half days and worked on my business for the rest of the week. By the end of the year I was making enough money to leave teaching and run the business full time.'

Karen

Before: Technology teacher

Now: On-line vintage clothing business

Lastly, you could take an interim job which would leave you with enough energy to begin working on your new career.

'I really wanted to become a counsellor and I began the course, but when it came to taking on clients, I found I was too tired and too preoccupied after a full day's teaching to really focus. A friend of mine who had his own business needed a driver so I left teaching and worked for him. Although I was working from eight till four, mentally it wasn't draining and I felt that the counselling was my 'real' job. It was a huge pay cut but enough to get by and I was grateful for it. Later I trained as a hypnotherapist and now I work full time at a hypnotherapy clinic.'
Will
Before: History teacher
Now: Hypnotherapist

Getting your family on side

For most people, leaving teaching isn't a decision that only affects them. You may have a partner, children, step children or other dependents. However much they might want you to be happier, if your decision to leave puts financial pressure on your partner, then it probably needs to be a joint decision. Whilst your children can probably adapt to fewer treats or holidays, if they were thinking you would be able to support them through university they may worry that they won't be able to afford it without your help and issues like this will need looking at. This is another reason why giving yourself time to plan ahead and explore alternatives would be better than handing in your notice too hastily.

Exercise 13
Writing you plan

Now that you have some idea of what you want to do, you would benefit from writing a plan. As with all good plans, this needs to be flexible and you may want to make changes to it as you go. Having an initial plan may take some of the fear factor out of the changes you are about to undertake and may help others see that you have given this careful thought and are in control.

Your plan can take any shape you like but I suggest you include the following information:

- Your eventual aim (e.g. I want to be a qualified hypnotherapist with my own business)
- A time scale
- The steps required to achieve this plan with a time frame for each step.
- A financial break down of your current assets, savings and earnings
- A financial forecast of the costs involved in your plan and a realistic estimate of income along the way.

- A contingency plan if things go wrong, or unexpected expenses arise.

If your plan involves staring your own business you will also need a full business plan. Useful advice and links to free templates can be found on the government website at https://www.gov.uk/write-business-plan.

Chapter Ten
What Ex-teachers Say

It takes a great deal of courage to give up a secure, well-paid job for the unknown of a new career however much you long to do it. You will inevitably worry and, as this book has been at pains to point out, you may well find yourself financially worse off, at least for a time. So what do ex-teachers say? The vast majority of ex-teachers whose stories have contributed to this book have a positive view of leaving teaching.

- 80% said their health, general well-being, family life and social life had improved
- 75% said their working conditions had improved
- 87% said they were less stressed

The positives have to be weighed up against the financial disadvantages. Only 25% of respondents said they were financially better off, 31% said they were about the same and 44% were financially worse off now than when they were teachers. Despite this, 97% said they were glad, overall, that they had left teaching. That's not to say that some don't have mixed feelings. Many ex-teachers would have liked to continue if only the job was different.

'I am glad I taught but I am sad about the current state of education and the lack of creativity.'
Lorie
Before: Science teacher
Now: Psychotherapist, supervisor and trainer

'I miss teaching itself and contact with the students. I don't miss the pressure, environment or lack of control of time. The current lack of money or security is sometimes scary but I know I could get supply if I was really desperate.'
Peter
Before: English teacher
Now: Website designer

'I have much more family time now. I would love to teach again but not under such stressful condition and with such a high work-load.'
Kim
Before: Primary school teacher
Now: Child minder

'I'm sad that I left a job that I loved because the hours and stress were incompatible with my family life.'
Meera
Before: Science teacher
Now: Assistant manager of clothes store

Others have no mixed feelings at all.

'I love the choices I have made which give me independence and freedom.'
Davina
Before: English and history teacher
Now: Private tutor

'I now wish I had left much sooner.'
Gordon
Before: Sixth form maths teacher
Now: IT trainer

'I'm relieved and I wouldn't return under any circumstances.'
Laura
Before: Home Economics teacher
Now: Wedding planner

'I have a much better quality of life now. I am far less stressed and I enjoy what I do.'
Chris
Before: Music teacher
Now: Private tutor

Final Word
This book is not meant to be an anti-teaching book. There is no intention to try to persuade people to leave a profession which is both essential and, in many cases, rewarding. It is simply an acknowledgement that, for many teachers, there is a shelf life to the job they do and neither they nor the students they teach will

benefit from their continuing in a job they no longer have a passion for.

Likewise this book is not meant to be a criticism of the current state of teaching (although, at times, that is difficult to avoid). It would be too easy to complain about long hours and immeasurable stress and argue that things should be different. The fact is that many thousands of teachers are very happy with their jobs and have been able to find the balance between work and family life. Each person is different and as our situations change we may find that something which once suited us, or which we once felt offered enough satisfaction to make the demands bearable, no longer fits that description.

This book is for anyone who wants to explore the possibility of leaving teaching. Teaching is not, after all, a life sentence.

Acknowledgements

I would like to thank all the teachers and ex-teachers who shared their stories, thoughts and feelings with me.

I would also like to thank my editorial team from 'Sam's Room Editorial Co' for their help, encouragement and technical know-how.

Clare Edwards

December 2014
leavingteachinguk@gmail.com

23507912R00074

Printed in Poland
by Amazon Fulfillment
Poland Sp. z o.o., Wrocław